CONNECTED TO CHRIST

CONNECTED TO CHRIST

Why Membership Matters

PETER SPECKHARD

CONCORDIA PUBLISHING HOUSE · SAINT LOUIS

2 3 4 5 6 7 8 9 10 11   26 25 24 23 22 21 20 19 18 17

CONTENTS

INTRODUCTION

The idea of membership has fallen on hard times these days. Many people prefer not to be "card-carrying members" of many organizations—or even any—and for good reason. While there are plenty of advantages involved in official membership, such as having a voice in the group's decisions and, in many cases, receiving benefits available only to members, there are some potential downsides too—some more serious than others. These downsides go beyond the simple give-and-take, such as the fact that you only have a voice if you go to meetings, or you only get benefits if you pay dues. No, the real downside with official membership is that it is risky for your reputation.

When you officially join a group or an organization, be it a fraternity, a political party, a civic club, or a charity, you share certain things—goals, money (in the form of contributions or dues), time—with the other people in that group. And in so doing, you also share a reputation. In a sense, you represent that organization wherever you go, and it can rightfully claim to represent you, at least partially, when it acts publicly. So, if there is anything remotely controversial or potentially unpopular about an organization, people tend to be shy about joining it even if they mostly agree with it.

Sure, anyone would be glad to officially be on the membership roster of a club dedicated to a popular and uncontroversial cause such as picking up litter or feeding poor children. We get a social boost by being associated with such groups. But what about politics, religion, or anything about which people might passionately disagree? No one wants to meet people at a dinner party or a barbecue and hear, "Oh, so you're one of *those* people." We don't want to be stereotyped by associations. We resent the assumptions people might make about us because of the groups to which we belong. So, we tend to be extremely guarded about membership. We might volunteer our time, appreciate others' efforts, or support their goals from afar, but seek official membership for ourselves? That's going a step too far for many of us.

Most traditional Christian congregations fall into this category of organizations that people, especially younger people, hesitate to join. Church membership and attendance have fallen sharply in the last few decades as many of those who grew up in these congregations have never made the transition to active adult members. Sit in on a Bible study at a traditional church and you will likely notice it mostly consists of older people. When they share their prayer requests, nearly all of them have on their hearts and minds a child, grandchild, or other relative who was raised in a church but has since stopped attending and let his or her membership lapse. Some of those younger people have transitioned into Christian groups or movements that do not bother with official membership. Some have perhaps stayed on the membership roll of their childhood church but rarely, if ever, attend. Some have let their membership lapse because they say church membership and attendance don't do anything for their faith. And some would no longer even claim to be Christian. Membership—formal, official belonging to a recognizable organization—simply doesn't seem like a priority anymore.

For Christians, there is good news and bad news when it comes to membership. The bad news is, you are a member of the Church whether you want to be or not. The good news? Membership in the Christian sense is unlike any other kind of membership.

Christians are by definition members of the Church, which is the people of God. We are baptized into a people, a kingdom, a body, a huge global family of Christians. To be a Christian is to be a member of a larger group. There is no such thing as Christianity that is simply one-on-one, you and Jesus, independent of other believers. You have a relationship with Jesus, of

> *There is no such thing as Christianity that is simply one-on-one, you and Jesus, independent of other believers.*

course, and in a sense, it is an extremely personal relationship—you know Him and He knows you. But that word personal, while true, is not exactly biblical and leaves out so much of what God gives us and how He forms us with the Gospel. Essentially, Christianity is corporate.

Consider how Jesus teaches us to pray in the Lord's Prayer. The first words are "Our Father." The plural is noteworthy and brings out a key point. If Jesus' only goal for your faith were merely for you to have a personal relationship with Him and God the Father, and if personal intimacy with God were the main point of His teachings on prayer, wouldn't He have taught you to pray, "My Father"? But He didn't do that in His Sermon on the Mount, and He still doesn't today. Your relationship to your heavenly Father is inextricably linked (though many try to extricate it) to your relationship to your brothers and sisters in Christ, your fellow believers. If you have Christ as King, you are part of a kingdom. If you have God as Father, you have brothers and sisters. You might not always get a chance to express

Essentially, Christianity is corporate.

that relationship to other believers, and as a sinner you might not express it very well even when you get the chance, but you have that relationship to other Christians simply by virtue of being a Christian yourself. God doesn't want you calling on Him as your Father if you refuse to acknowledge the rest of His family as your family. Jesus won't allow you to claim a relationship with God as His child while disavowing your relationship to your fellow believers, as His teachings on prayer and His parables make clear.

Refresh your memory of the parable of the prodigal son by looking it up in Luke 15:11–32. In this parable about God's grace, look at the little verbal trick of misdirection that the resentful older brother tries to use on his father. Complaining to his father about the party for his ne'er-do-well younger brother, the older brother says, "But when *this son of yours* came, who has devoured your property with prostitutes, you killed the fattened calf for him!" (v. 30, emphasis added). But the father (who in the parable represents God) quickly turns it back on the older brother by saying, "It was fitting to celebrate and be glad, for this *your brother* was dead, and is alive; he was lost, and is found" (v. 32, emphasis added). Notice the italicized words, especially the pronouns *yours* and *your*. The older brother wants to claim his own sonship while downplaying or denying his relationship with the younger brother. But the father doesn't let him get away with it. His words remind the older brother that because the older brother is the father's son, so all of the father's sons are brothers to one another, and they cannot get out of it just because they don't like it.

There is no use trying to be connected to God without being connected to the rest of His family, no matter how much some of those family members may drive you nuts. God won't disavow His other children for your sake any more than He would ever disown you for theirs. If, when you were a child, your parents had another child, you weren't in a position to decide whether you wanted to officially be a brother or sister. You may have acted like you were in such a position, but you soon found out you really weren't. You were only in a position to decide how good of a brother or sister to be. That is the case as well in the family of God. All Christians are a group; the challenge for each individual Christian is how to acknowledge, express, and realize that fact.

All Christians are a group; the challenge for each individual Christian is how to acknowledge, express, and realize that fact.

CHAPTER 1

TWO TYPES OF MEMBERSHIP

Membership takes many forms, but all of them fall roughly into two categories. The first type of membership consists of many identical or similar things collected together. For example, an individual brick might serve as a doorstop or bookend, but bricks serve their individual purpose best when collected together. A few thousand bricks all together can make a wall, which is the real purpose of bricks. Despite whatever differences make each brick unique, bricks are more or less interchangeable with one another; however, each brick fulfills its purpose best when used collectively. A bag of marbles, a design made of tumbling dominoes, a stack of dollar bills—all of those things represent collective membership, the kind of membership in which an individual thing achieves its purpose better as a member of a larger group of basically similar things.

The other kind of membership is organic, which means the individual members are not interchangeable but together form an interdependent whole. A rock band might have four or five members, but the bass player is not the same as the drummer. The lead singer cannot necessarily stand in for the lead guitarist. They are all members of the band, but four drummers do not normally make up a rock band, nor do four bass guitarists. In organic membership, the whole is greater than the sum of its parts, and each part is more dependent on its relationship with the whole to achieve its purpose. The members' differences play a crucial role in the larger unity of the thing of which they are all members.

Most collections of people take on aspects of both kinds of membership. In certain ways, a group of soldiers might be interchangeable parts of a larger whole, say, when charging a hill or marching in a parade. But in other ways, the group exhibits aspects of organic membership, as the unit made of snipers, scouts, medics, and supply drivers achieves a mission in which each member plays a distinct, interdependent role. The same might be said of a marching band; in one sense, it consists of a collection of more or less interchangeable members making up a pattern on the field. But in another sense, each instrumentalist plays a different set of notes that together make up the harmonious melody.

So, which kind of membership is church membership? Like most groups involving many people, church membership is both collective and organic. In terms of church attendance or the size of a particular congregation, one hundred church members amount to one church member a hundred times over, like a hundred bricks in a wall or a hundred dominoes in a line. Expressed statistically, church membership is merely the collective kind of membership. But the biblical reality focuses far more on the organic kind of membership, as we'll see in a moment in the words of St. Paul. Even in a family with many children, each child is a unique part of the whole family. While Christians quite properly claim to be the family of God, the biblical idea of what unifies us goes much further.

In addition to the idea of a family, St. Paul uses the metaphor of one body with many parts to describe the relationship each Christian has with Jesus Christ and with other Christians. "Now you are the body of Christ and individually members of it" (1 Corinthians 12:27). It's hard to get more plain and direct than that. Christians are a collective whole and ought to recognize that fact. Christ is the head. The head controls each member and harmonizes all the movements and functions of the whole body. Each Christian is like one member of the body—a foot, an eye, an ear, and so on—who serves the head, Christ, but only does so in concert with the other members. St. Paul leads up to the frank declaration that you are a member of the body whether you like it or not with a more detailed explanation:

> For just as the body is one and has many members, and
> all the members of the body, though many, are one body,

so it is with Christ. For in one Spirit we were all baptized into one body—Jews or Greeks, slaves or free—and all were made to drink of one Spirit. For the body does not consist of one member but of many. If the foot should say, "Because I am not a hand, I do not belong to the body," that would not make it any less a part of the body. And if the ear should say, "Because I am not an eye, I do not belong to the body," that would not make it any less a part of the body. If the whole body were an eye, where would be the sense of hearing? If the whole body were an ear, where would be the sense of smell? But as it is, God arranged the members in the body, each one of them, as He chose. If all were a single member, where would the body be? As it is, there are many parts, yet one body. The eye cannot say to the hand, "I have no need of you," nor again the head to the feet, "I have no need of you." On the contrary, the parts of the body that seem to be weaker are indispensable, and on those parts of the body that we think less honorable we bestow the greater honor, and our unpresentable parts are treated with greater modesty, which our more presentable parts do not require. But God has so composed the body, giving greater honor to the part that lacked it, that there may be no division in the body, but that the members may have the same care for one another. If one member suffers, all suffer together; if one member is honored, all rejoice together. (1 Corinthians 12:12–26)

You can apply St. Paul's metaphor to yourself quite easily. Wiggle your left thumb. If you can do that, then you know that your left thumb has a relationship with your head and mind. Your thumb does what your brain tells it to do. If it doesn't, then your thumb itself or its relationship to your brain is impaired. But if you have no trouble moving your left thumb, then your thumb is healthy and the relationship between it and your brain is good.

But here is the key: if you cut your thumb off from your hand, you also cut it off from your brain. Your thumb has no relationship to your brain apart from a relationship with your hand, wrist, arm, nerves, muscles, veins, and the rest of your body. A thumb cannot serve the brain while remaining apart from the body. That is the whole point of St. Paul's metaphor. A Christian is not called simply to an individual and personal relationship with God in Christ Jesus. A Christian is called to be a living, working part of the corporate body of Christ. The personal relationship and the corporate membership are two sides of the same coin, inextricably linked. "Corporate" really just means "bodily" or

A Christian is called to be a living, working part of the corporate body of Christ. The personal relationship and the corporate membership are two sides of the same coin, inextricably linked.

"as a body" and refers to many individuals acting as one, but each contributing uniquely to the work of the whole body. Just as no body part can be a living member of the body without having a relationship with the head, so no Christian can have a relationship with Christ, the head, without being a living member of the body, the Church.

All the parts of the body are supposed to work together to achieve the goals set by the brain. Consider what some people say is the hardest thing to do in all of professional sports: hitting a baseball. To pull it off, your feet, legs, and hips have to maintain perfect balance while your shoulders, arms, and wrists swing the bat with all their might. All the while, your eyes must stay absolutely fixed on the speeding ball. Your whole body must be disciplined enough to obey your brain precisely while it triggers each separate movement to coordinate with the rest. But what if your eyes lose focus? Even if you maintain perfect balance and execute your best swing, you will miss the ball. Without your eyes, your hands can't play baseball. Nor can your shoulders or feet. That whole goal of the brain is thwarted for the whole body. And the same would be true if the eyes stayed and the hands left.

St. Paul does not tell Christians they should seriously consider becoming members of the Church, the Body of Christ. He says we are members, whether we like it or not. In other words, for Christians, the question is not whether to be members of the body. The question is how we can best be effective, functioning members. Every Christian has an intimate relationship with every other Christian simply by having a relationship with Christ.

While that all sounds great, the question remains: how formal or organized does that membership have to be? Christ can "organize" or coordinate and use Christians in ways not visible to us. Maybe we can all work together in conjunction with His plan despite not having any formal relationship with one another. At any rate, one thing no one can deny is that not all Christians are members of the same congregation or denomination. Still, some will ask: can't we recognize other Christians as our brothers and sisters in Christ without formally putting our names on the list of official members of this or that congregation or denomination? Sure, we could. But is that the most effective way of being a member of the Body?

Every Christian has an intimate relationship with every other Christian simply by having a relationship with Christ.

The real issue to consider is what makes us hesitant to join a church. Why wouldn't we join a church? While it's true that no official list of members of one denomination or church can claim to be the official list of Christians in the world, is that a reason to reject the idea of membership to such an organization? St. Paul's words should make all Christians realize more and more how essential to the faith it is to recognize our membership with other living, breathing, imperfect Christians. We do that most effectively when we outwardly acknowledge the spiritual connection we have with one another, which is what congregations and denominations seek to do.

Many people today, even those who think of themselves as Christian believers, reject this truth, to the church's and their own great loss. You've probably heard many people say something along the lines of, "I'm a spiritual person, but I don't believe in organized religion." You might have even said that yourself at one time or another. It is a common enough sentiment to be a cliché. But like many common statements, it says deceptively little when you press it for genuine meaning. And for Christians, it actually makes no sense to reject "organized religion" once we realize Christianity is inherently organized, meaning that by its very divine design, it calls us to membership in a larger body. The body is organic, that is, it has different members or organs working interdependently as one. To be a member of a living body is to be organized. Certainly to be a Christian is to be organized. So let's look at what that common sentiment really means in light of God's Word.

PART 1: "I'm a Spiritual Person, . . ."

Of course you are. People are by definition spiritual in that they have a spirit. That's what people are: bodies and spirits together. ("Soul" sometimes is used interchangeably with "spirit" but can also more technically refer to the life of the body and spirit together.) You may as well say, "I'm a biological person." Of course you are biological. And of course you are spiritual. Everyone is. But there is a big difference between a live person and a corpse, even though both of them have a body. And there is a big difference between someone who is spiritually alive in Christ and someone who is spiritually dead and not connected to Christ by faith, even though both of them have a spirit. When the Bible speaks of "you who are spiritual" (Galatians 6:1), it is referring to those whose spirits have been made alive through faith in Christ.

Most people would probably say that by claiming to be spiritual, they mean much more than that they simply have a spirit. So what do they mean? That they're aware they have a spirit? That their soul matters to them? Most likely it means something like "I'm a spiritually alive person." But then we have to ask ourselves if saying so makes it so. St. Paul said that a member—for example, an eye or an ear—remains a member even when it says it isn't, though maybe not a cooperative or functional member. So what about a non-member, someone without faith in Christ who hasn't been baptized into Him, claiming to be spiritually alive? Does claiming it make it so? What or who is the source of spiritual life?

God's Word is clear: we were originally designed to be live bodies and live spirits together in one living person, but because of the fall into sin, mankind's spirit died. We are born spiritually dead, that is, slaves to sin. Only our connection to God by faith in Jesus Christ awakens that part of us to genuine spiritual life. In Romans 6:13, St. Paul tells Christians to "present yourselves to God as those who have been brought from death to life." In Ephesians 2, he tells us that we were dead in our trespasses and sins, but God in His great love and mercy "made us alive together with Christ" (v. 5). And in many other places throughout Scripture, the idea is the same; we've gone from slavery to freedom, blindness to having sight, lost to being found, dead to living—but always and only by God's grace through faith in Jesus Christ. Apart from that, we remain enslaved, lost, blind, and dead, no matter how spiritual we feel ourselves to be.

So if people claim to be spiritual or spiritually alive, that can only mean they have faith in Christ, in which case they are Christians. Otherwise, they are mistaken, since no one without faith can please God with their meditations, good deeds, spiritual feelings, or religious observances.

This observation is a great scandal, of course. Jesus, St. Paul, Martin Luther, and Christians through the ages have had to acknowledge the difficult truth that Christianity makes exclusive claims. Christianity can never be one acceptable religion among others. Consider what Roman Catholic writer G. K. Chesterton said about Christianity's claim to exclusivity: "Nobody understands the nature of the Church, or the ringing note of the creed descending from antiquity, who does not realize that the whole world once very nearly died of broadmindedness and the brotherhood of all religions" (G. K. Chesterton, The Everlasting Man [San Francisco: Ignatius Press, 1993], 178). At first, this quote sounds absurd. But the more you explore the idea behind it, the more sense it makes. Chesterton rooted the whole issue of whether many and contradictory

Jesus, St. Paul, Martin Luther, and Christians through the ages have had to acknowledge the difficult truth that Christianity makes exclusive claims.

religions could all be equally valid, quite rightly, in the Old Testament. Pagans all had their local gods, and when the people came into contact with one another and formed larger nations and empires, they pooled their gods and filled Pantheons with them. Everyone's god fit in somewhere; it wasn't as though the Egyptians thought their gods existed and the Persian gods did not. It was that their gods were *theirs* and the Persian gods were not—they could all coexist and get along if need be. The Greeks and Romans simply took all the various gods they encountered and said they were all part of the same grand, heavenly world.

The God of Israel, by way of contrast, refused to ever share His throne with any other god. He claimed He was the only God and the rightful God of everyone. All other worship, even of angels, was idolatry. All other gods were imposters, demons, or inventions of people. But even the Israelites created gods, which inverted the relationship of Creator and creation.

When Queen Jezebel married King Ahab of Israel, she offered an enlightened and tolerant solution to the problem of two nations with differing religious traditions sharing the same space. She simply brought her god, Baal, with her and set up her people's god for worship alongside the God of Israel (1 Kings 16). The prophet Elijah (who today would be labeled a narrow-minded, intolerant zealot), refused to allow it. His message was the original, "There can be only one" (see 1 Kings 18). And the same has been true of Christians from day one. Back in the days of the Roman Empire, believers in any and every religion, or no religion at all, had to offer a pinch of incense to Caesar acknowledging his divinity. These people didn't have to believe it, they just had to bow to Caesar. The right people, the people with a future, the enlightened and tolerant, all figured that it didn't matter much and doing so without protest would help everybody get along. The Christians, however, insisted they would rather be tortured to death than do any such thing.

This might seem like an insignificant point, but it makes a huge difference. Imagine the God of Abraham, Isaac, and Jacob taking His place in a pantheon or family of other gods and goddesses. The Jewish God who revealed Himself as the Christian God would have simply become a pagan myth and died out along with all the other pagan gods whom no one believes in anymore. The Christian God is not the last of the Olympians, persisting long after everyone stopped believing in Zeus; but that is because God never dwelt on Olympus— He was never just one of several equally valid pagan gods. It was critical, absolutely necessary, for the God of Israel to be understood not as one god among many but as *the* God. Nothing else would make sense in the long run. Jesus, as the Son of *the* God, is not a way, a truth, and a life, but *the* Way, *the* Truth, and *the* Life. And as He added to those claims, "No one comes to the Father except through Me" (John 14:6). Again, this claim scandalizes the world, especially for those who cannot see any crucial, essential differences between religions and would prefer not to let any such differences divide people.

Of course, none of this means Christians can coerce anyone into becoming a believer in Christ. That is impossible. And none of this means Christians should be rude or nasty to people of other religions, or that we can't be good neighbors to them. No modern nation is the theological equivalent of ancient Israel. Unlike Elijah, we do indeed have to share space with worshipers of other gods. The exclusive claims of Christ simply mean that one cannot accept the claims of Christianity and also accept the claims of any non-Christian religion when they contradict the Truth as revealed in Christ.

If nothing else, the world's rejection of the scandalous

claim that salvation is only found in Christ shows that the common complaints against Christians today are not recent phenomena. Because Christians have refused—and continue to refuse—to acknowledge every religion as equally valid, they are considered narrow-minded and intolerant. They are reminded that their constant evangelism efforts make it harder for people to coexist, and that their confidence in Christ amounts to bigotry against non-Christians. These criticisms were happening a century ago, a millennium ago, and even two and three millennia ago. Nothing has changed in that regard.

> *It remains as important today as it was in Elijah's and Jezebel's day that Christians realize the Church was, is, and until Judgement Day will be, a scandal to the world.*

It remains as important today as it was in Elijah's and Jezebel's day that Christians realize the Church was, is, and until Judgment Day will be, a scandal to the world. But the scandal of Christ is a necessary, salvific scandal, not put there to be mean and bigoted but to shine light into the darkness. Being connected to Christ by faith is what makes us spiritually alive. And if we are connected to Him, we are connected to one another, and ought to recognize this fact.

PART 2:

" . . . but I Don't Believe in Organized Religion."

Now let's look at the second part of that cliché, the part about not believing in organized religion. Here is where the fundamental fact that Christians are members of the Church whether they want to be or not really shows up. People have this idea that one's faith or religion is personal and private—that it is a matter of opinion and therefore more like a personal philosophy. Joining an organization is simply getting together with like-minded people, which some may wish to do, and others may not. You can be the biggest fan of your favorite team, but you may or may not decide to become an official member of the team's fan club. Fandom is different from fan club membership. Whether you do or don't join the club doesn't change your status as a fan; it isn't as though the people who don't join the official fan club aren't really fans.

Christianity is not like a Jesus fan club. But that's how many people view organized religion. They see it as a bunch of like-minded people forming an official club. By this view, whether you join the official club of Christians at a local church or decide not to join doesn't have much

> Christianity is not like a Jesus fan club. But that's how many people view organized religion.

of an effect on your own personal faith. As we've seen, however, that idea doesn't work well in the case of Christianity. The Church isn't just a group of like-minded individuals; it is individual members who form a body. So, saying you are a Christian but not an official member of a Christian church is really like saying you are a dedicated baseball player but don't believe in organized team sports. You might be a great baseball player in terms of your skills and knowledge of the game, but if you aren't actually on a team, then in at least one very important sense, you aren't a baseball player at all.

Objections abound. Some will say, "Look at all the terrible things the Church has done through the years. I don't want any part of that. I'm a Christian, but I don't want to lend my support to oppression and religious wars and all that." By all means, don't. While the crimes of the Church tend to be greatly overstated by her critics, the visible, organized Church has been unquestionably responsible for acts that betrayed her Lord. An organization full of sinners will inevitably do bad things and must repent

Saying you are a Christian but not an official member of a Christian church is really like saying you are a dedicated baseball player but don't believe in organized team sports.

and seek forgiveness. No one said the Church—whether at the congregational, national, or global level—always lived up to its identity as the holy people of God. As someone once said, the Church is like Noah's Ark—nobody in it would put up with the stink if it weren't for the nature of the alternatives.

"But," the critics continue, "there are so many different churches and denominations. If the Christian Church is one big family, one Body of Christ, then shouldn't there only be one of them in any given town? If all Christians are supposed to be members of a congregation, how are they supposed to know which congregation to join?" These are excellent questions, questions that many people ponder and that keep them from ever being comfortable with the idea of official membership in a church.

One of the greatest scandals, perhaps the greatest scandal (scandal means "stumbling block," something that trips people up or gives offense), that hurts the Christian witness to the world is the fact that Christians themselves are divided when Scripture tells us not to be. First Corinthians 1:10–13 says,

> I appeal to you, brothers, by the name of our Lord Jesus Christ, that all of you agree, and that there be no divisions among you, but that you be united in the same mind and the same judgment. For it has been reported to me by Chloe's people that there is quarreling among you,

my brothers. What I mean is that each one of you says, "I follow Paul," or "I follow Apollos," or "I follow Cephas," or "I follow Christ." Is Christ divided? Was Paul crucified for you? Or were you baptized in the name of Paul?

This passage represents one of many that teach the same thing. Clearly Christians ought not divide themselves. They ought to agree.

> One of the greatest scandals, perhaps the greatest scandal, that hurts the Christian witness to the world is the fact that Christians themselves are divided when Scripture tells us not to be.

How can we talk of unity, family, and one body if many different churches of various denominations all claim to be Christian? The fact that a Christian is by definition a member of a body or family but that same Christian is confronted by disunity, divisions, and competing choices as to what church to join is indeed shameful and proof that Christians remain sinners in this world. It should not be like that. Imagine how glorious it would be if the children of God dwelt together in unity.

But the problem of a divided church is difficult to solve. It isn't just a matter of ignoring the differences or claiming they don't matter. Anyone who explores the differences between the denominations in any depth finds that the differences in what they teach do indeed make a big difference. They can't just be papered over. On the other hand, no one can say that the true children of God are limited to one denomination, as though there were no Christians in the other denominations. However, St. Paul did not recommend unity with those who taught something other than the Gospel as the apostles taught it. He began his Letter to the Galatians by saying,

> I am astonished that you are so quickly deserting Him who called you in the grace of Christ and are turning to a different gospel—not that there is another one, but there are some who trouble you and want to distort the gospel of Christ. But even if we or an angel from heaven should preach to you a gospel contrary to the one we preached to you, let him be accursed. (Galatians 1:6–8)

With these words, St. Paul acknowledges that false teaching disrupts the unity of the Church, and sadly, even Christians are prone to follow false teachers.

The effort to achieve unity in the Christian Church is ongoing. It is called ecumenism, and most church leaders are involved in various ways, trying to figure out how the Christian Church can be united without compromising crucial aspects of Christianity. Unity is something Christians pray for. The goal of ecumenism is to make the visible, worldly organization of the Church—the membership lists, parish boundaries, lines of accountability, official positions, and all that sort of thing—correlate as closely as possible to the spiritual reality that everyone who has faith in Jesus Christ is really a member of one living Body.

In the meantime, every Christian has to decide which church to join. The best way to make that decision is to look at what exactly unites Christians. Christians are not united by ethnicity, economic class, political leanings, education level, or any other distinction the world uses to categorize people. The Church transcends every human category. It includes young and old, rich and poor, black and white, male and female, people of every tribe and language who are united by nothing but Christ. The source of our unity is Christ and our faith in Him. False teaching makes for a false church, but a sound confession of faith perpetuates the Church and its mission. Therefore, the number one thing, really the only thing that ought to determine which church a person joins is that church's teaching, its public doctrine or confession of faith.

> *The most important consideration as to what church to join is its confession of faith.*

The Christian Church is sometimes compared to a flock of sheep. Jesus calls Himself the Good Shepherd. Martin Luther called the Christian Church "lambs who hear the voice of their Shepherd" (Smalcald Articles, Part III, Article XII, paragraphs 2–3). So when a Christian today joins a church, he or she must ask, "Am I able to listen to this confession of faith, as preached and taught, as the voice of the Shepherd? Can I submit to it? Am I willing to be corrected and admonished by those who hold this confession of faith? Or am I really remaining unconnected, a free agent merely observing and critiquing the teachings as something to consider, and taking or leaving them as I see fit?" If you are part of the latter group—if you really don't allow yourself to be corrected by the teachings of your church body—then you aren't hearing the voice of your Shepherd in that place and aren't fully a part of the flock, the family.

Conclusion

The prospective church member must ask, "Does this church truly and fully preach and teach Christ and offer Christ in the Sacraments according to His biblical commands?" We'll look at those things more in the next chapter, but for now, the key point is that the confession of faith is what matters about a church. And mutual faith is what unites people. Many people are tempted to join a church because it has a dynamic preacher, great music, friendly

The confession of faith is what matters about a church. And mutual faith is what unites people.

people, comfortable seats, convenient service times, or even good coffee. But far more important than any of those things is what it teaches. Are you willing to be taught, and even corrected, by the teachings of this church body? A boring pastor shuffling around and droning on and on about Christ crucified is far better than a dynamic pastor offering practical, "real world" wisdom and miraculous signs. "Jews demand signs and Greeks seek wisdom, but we preach Christ crucified, a stumbling block to Jews and folly to Gentiles" (1 Corinthians 1:22–23).

You have to make the decision for yourself and always have the final say in which church you are going to be a part of. But you also then have to consent to be corrected and taught by your church in recognition that your own discernment of true teaching is not always sufficient. Therefore, there is a "which came first, the chicken or the egg?" dilemma for

> *There is a "which came first, the chicken or the egg?" dilemma for new Christians when it comes to deciding what church to join.*

new Christians when it comes to deciding what church to join. On one hand, you have to know what you believe in order to evaluate a church's confession of faith. On the other hand, you have to be taught by a church and its confession of faith, always comparing that confession with God's Word, in order to know what God says and therefore what you believe. So do you pick a church first and accept its teachings, or do you somehow determine true teaching first and then find a church that teaches it? Tough questions, to be sure, and hopefully the rest of this book will help you answer them. For now, suffice to say that the difficulty of sorting this out is no justification for pretending it must not matter. Which confession of faith you allow to teach and correct you matters more than which doctor does your heart surgery or who is in charge of your retirement accounts. Disagreements and divisions make it harder for people to decide, but they do not remove the need for decision.

CHAPTER 2

THE PURPOSE OF CHURCH

When you're deciding which church to join or whether to join a church at all, or when you have recently joined a church or have been a member of a congregation for many decades, you have to confront the relationship between church membership and the church service itself. The church service is the heart and soul of living the faith. What breathing and heartbeats are to the life of the body, Word and Sacrament as offered in worship are to the life of the Church. Yes, most churches have many activities and programs beyond the church service. While one congregation operates a homeless shelter, another hosts addiction support groups, another helps refugees resettle in their community, another assists at a crisis pregnancy center, and another's youth group partners with nursing homes to brighten the days of the elderly. There are hundreds of such opportunities, plus all the purely social activities such as church softball leagues, quilting clubs, and so forth. However, none of those activities—great as they may be—are the main point of a congregation. Helping others, especially the most helpless, is critical for Christians to do, and building relationships through social events is certainly helpful too. But non-Christian clubs do similar activities as well. When congregations do those important things, they aren't necessarily doing anything unique to Christian congregations. What happens in the church service itself, however, is not only the most important thing about church membership, but it is also something that happens nowhere else except in the context of the church service.

> *What happens in the church service itself, however, is not only the most important thing about church membership, but it is also something that happens nowhere else except in the context of the church service.*

When you walk out of church, how do you know whether the service was good or not? To answer that question, you have to know what you were going there for in the first place. The service can only be evaluated according to its purpose. This is true of anything, really. You can judge the places you go—restaurants, gas stations, movies, doctors' offices, beauty salons, auto mechanics, hotels, used car lots, you name it—only according to their purpose. People might say the movie was great because it kept them on the edge of their seat, but nobody says it was a great trip to the dentist because it kept them on the edge of their seat. Movie theaters and dentists' offices serve different purposes for us. We expect different things out of them. We typically know why we go to the dentist, or to the gym, or to the hardware store, so we typically have no problem evaluating whether it was a successful trip. But many Christians simply don't know the purpose of going to church.

When people don't understand the purpose of the church service, they either stop attending altogether or they attend sporadically for incidental and personal reasons such as family tradition, the comfort of familiarity, the connection to their "church friends," or a number of other reasons. Of course, when you use those reasons for going to church, you can easily determine whether it was a good service. For some people, the service gets an A-plus because it was short and there were a lot of people there they knew, so the fellowship was great. Others perhaps rate the service highly because it included

Many Christians simply don't know the purpose of going to church.

their favorite hymns or songs, while others give it bad reviews because the music was unfamiliar. For some people, the service was great because the music absolutely rocked or the sermon was so moving it made them cry, or it was lame because the sermon was really boring. In all of these cases, people have evaluated the service based on something tangential to its purpose, which is like saying the trip to the auto mechanic was bad because the coffee in the waiting room was cold. Cold coffee may be a bummer, but shouldn't we evaluate a trip to the auto mechanic according to how well they fixed the car? That was, after all, the purpose of the trip.

The purpose of attending a Christian church service is to be served by Jesus Christ through the Word and Sacrament. At its heart, this service is spiritual. It can at times provide an emotional, intellectual, or psychological experience for people too. But giving such gifts is not the primary goal of the service. The main purpose of the service is forgiving your sins, strengthening your faith, and bringing you into the presence of God, which may or may not strike you emotionally or intellectually on any given day but definitely impact you spiritually when you receive the gifts in faith. Those are all interdependent things, like one thing expressed in three different ways or three strands intertwined into one rope. The strength of the strands in that rope determines how well the service fulfilled its purpose.

The reason it is so difficult to keep the real purpose of the church service central to your experience is that you can't see it or prove it is happening. Like virtually everything in the Christian life, it is a matter of faith, not sight. You can judge a restaurant by tasting the food. You can evaluate your trip to the barbershop by looking in a mirror. And we're all tempted to judge our Sunday morning trip to church on similar, tangible, worldly criteria. But you can't watch the Holy Spirit work through the preaching, nor can you see God with anything but the eyes of faith when you come into His presence. You can't feel your sins being forgiven. You can only trust His promise that it is so. Faith, not sight, is what receives the gifts given in worship, and going by feelings is another way of going by sight rather than by faith.

The purpose of attending a Christian church service is to be served by Jesus Christ through the Word and Sacrament.

So a "bad" church service is not one that is boring, or one that features unfamiliar songs or lousy music, or one in which you don't know or feel connected to any of the other worshipers. Granted, the service is better if the sermon isn't boring, the music is good, and you know the others there, just as it is better if the coffee in the mechanic's waiting room is hot and tasty. Most churches recognize the importance of these tangential things and how poor execution can place unnecessary roadblocks in the way of people hearing the Word. But it's important that those tangible or even emotional things remain tangential; they aren't the main point. A "bad" service preaches and teaches things that aren't true to God's Word, or doesn't focus on Christ and the forgiveness He won, or focuses on the worshipers and what they do rather than letting them be served by God's grace. Every trip to church is successful as long as it offers or assures you of the forgiveness of sins, strengthens your faith in Christ by preaching Christ crucified, and brings you spiritually into the presence of God. That's how Jesus serves you.

When you know the purpose of the service, you realize you go to church more to be acted on than to act. What a massage does for your tight muscles or the dentist does for your teeth, a church service does for your spirit. In other words, it is basically more passive than active. Something is happening *to* you rather than requiring something *from* you. The direction of the service, the main flow of action, is from God to you. You cooperate, of course, by listening attentively, singing, and praying, just as you cooperate with the dentist by opening wide, but the main thrust of the church service moves from God to the assembled people. It is called a church "service" primarily because in it God serves us.

When you know the purpose of the service, you realize you go to church more to be acted on than to act.

When we remember that God is the one who is active in the service and that it is His way of serving us, then we realize that the service is about what is actually happening in the here and now, not just about what happened on Calvary two thousand years ago right outside Jerusalem. To be sure, the crucifixion and resurrection of Christ that happened centuries ago in a very specific time and place are absolutely central to Christianity. But the church service is not simply a celebration of that event. The church service is the setting in which God gives the very real results of that event to you and makes Christ's death and resurrection something that is "for you" here and now. This distinction may seem trivial, but it makes a big difference in terms of what we expect from the service and how we approach it.

Think about the difference between a wedding and a wedding reception. The wedding itself is generally formal and ceremonial. It comes across as ritualistic. Everyone there already knows basically what is going to happen in the wedding service, but they treat it as important because something momentous is actually happening in front of them. Guests dress up. They sit still and listen attentively despite the lack of surprises. The setting matters to people; they want the building or outdoor setting to be traditional or striking and beautiful.

The reception, however, is typically far more casual and celebratory; it is *about* the wedding. It is not the wedding itself. There is still a general format to the occasion, but the spirit or atmosphere is upbeat, informal, and the reception's success or failure depends very much on how "into it" people get, as any DJ or band can attest. As long as the entertainment has a place to set up, the reception can happen just as well in a convention center or some other purely utilitarian setting.

Christian worship through the centuries has quite right-fully been more like a wedding (formal and ceremonial) than a wedding reception (casual and celebratory), because the Christian service focuses on Christ crucified as proclaimed and offered in the Word and Sacrament. The gifts of Christ come in the worship service. It isn't just a celebration of something that happened long ago. Thus, churches that focus on the gifts given in worship will naturally (and quite properly) tend to have more formal ceremony or ritual in their services, while churches that focus less on the gifts given in the service, the Word and Sacraments, will tend to offer services with an atmosphere more like a wedding reception, focusing far more on our actions and our praise of God. The success of such services tends to depend more on whether people "get into it" or not, so such services sometimes reverse the direction of the service entirely, as though the worshipers are not there to receive God's gifts but merely to celebrate having them.

The Christian service focuses on Christ crucified as proclaimed and offered in the Word and Sacrament.

Many people naturally prefer the casual atmosphere of the reception to the "stiff" or "stuffy" atmosphere of a ceremony. That means worship focused on giving Christ in Word and Sacraments to receptive worshipers will often feel foreign, disappoint new members on the "get into it" scale of successful worship, and seem too old-fashioned for people's tastes. The best thing church members can do in that case is to realize why things are the way they are in a church service. Christ proclaimed in the Scriptures and sermon and offered in Holy Communion feeds our souls with the bread of life.

One Service, Two Parts: Word and Sacrament

So what is happening, and what is the typical person's role in the worship service? While congregations differ in the particulars, generally a worship service consists of two parts of equal importance, like the two lenses of a pair of glasses, both focused on Christ. The first is called the Service of the Word and features Scripture readings, hymns, preaching, a confession of faith, and prayers. The second part is called the Service of the Sacrament and features all of the aspects of receiving the body and blood of Christ—the fruit of His sacrifice on the cross—via Holy Communion.

> For I received from the Lord what I also delivered to you, that the Lord Jesus on the night when He was betrayed took bread, and when He had given thanks, He broke it, and said, "This is My body which is for you. Do this in remembrance of Me." In the same way also He took the cup, after supper, saying, "This cup is the new covenant in My blood. Do this, as you often as you drink it, in remembrance of Me." (1 Corinthians 11:23–25)

So those two things—the Word, Christ crucified in Scripture and proclaimed in the sermon, and the Sacrament—are the two main things with which God serves His people in worship.

The order of service varies from place to place and by denomination, but there are broad similarities across churches. The following description of what happens in worship and why it does pertains to a traditional Lutheran congregation, but most traditional Episcopalians, Presbyterians, Roman Catholics, Orthodox, and many others will probably find it fairly familiar if not exact.

PART 1: **Service of the Word**

Before the service begins, there is usually some time given for the worshipers to prepare. This time might be used to pray for the congregation, the pastor, or some personal concern (many hymnals have suggested preservice prayers printed in them) and, especially, to examine the state of one's own faith and life, which is part of the process of receiving Holy Communion.

In many services, either right before the service or near the very beginning of the service, there is a brief order of Confession and Absolution, in which the worshiper, like the prophet Isaiah, confesses that he or she is unworthy to come into the presence of the holy, living God. After witnessing the heavenly worship of God, Isaiah cries out, "Woe is me! For I am lost; for I am a man of unclean lips, and I dwell in the midst of a people of unclean lips; for my eyes have seen the King, the Lord of hosts!" (Isaiah 6:5). But then an angel touches Isaiah's lips with a live coal from the altar and says, "Your guilt is taken away, and your sin atoned for" (Isaiah 6:7). Forgiveness enables the sinful, impure Isaiah to come into God's presence. In the same way, by pure, unmerited grace for Christ's sake, God, speaking through the pastor, declares those sins and impurities in the worshipers' hearts to have been wiped away, forgiven, erased. This Confession and Absolution sets the stage for the interaction between God and His people that happens in the worship service.

Normally the next part is what is called an Introit. Don't worry about funny words and names you encounter in a church service. You learn such terms gradually, and knowing the precise term isn't what is important anyway; all it means is "entrance song." The Introit consists of sung, chanted, or spoken verses from the Psalms that usually have to do with the people entering into the temple courts. The idea is that just as God, in the Old Testament, dwelt in the Most Holy Place in the temple and people chanted these Psalms as they approached His presence, so we today, who now understand the verses as having been fulfilled in Christ, enter into God's presence in the sanctuary. As you sing or ponder these words, remember that you are coming to stand before God as a forgiven sinner. Remember also that it is only by faith, not by sight, that the realities of the worship service can be known.

The next part is usually a hymn, song, or canticle (again, the distinction between these isn't all that critical and will become clear with regular worship) that is all about praising God. It often begins with the words of Luke 2:14, when the angel host appears to the shepherds, saying, "Glory to God in the highest, and on earth peace among those with whom He is pleased!"; but it can take a whole host of forms. The main point is that this is the part of the service that is purely "praise" amid many other parts of the service. Such praise is the natural reaction to knowing God—simply lauding, honoring, glorifying, and praising Him for all His glory, including the mercy that allows sinners like us to join in the song.

It is only by faith, not by sight, that the realities of the worship service can be known.

Next, there is typically a short prayer called a Collect, pronounced not the normal way but instead with the emphasis on the first syllable. This is also sometimes called the Prayer of the Day. This prayer expresses the basic, central theme of the service. It is important to remember that in times of prayer, the worshiper is to be praying, not evaluating the text of the prayer or critiquing the one leading the congregation in prayer. The worshiper is not there to observe but to participate, which he or she does by praying even when others supply the words and voice of the congregation's prayer.

Next there are readings from Scripture, usually one from the Old Testament, one from the New Testament Epistles, and then a reading from one of the four Gospels. The Scriptures are God's written Word for us, and these readings focus on Christ throughout salvation history. Thus, the Scriptures form the foundation for everything that is taught and preached in a Christian service.

Following the Gospel reading, worshipers often sing the Hymn of the Day, which is usually based on some aspect of the Gospel reading. Then, the pastor delivers his sermon, which proclaims Christ according to that same Gospel theme. These three elements of the service are usually all interconnected and form the climax of the Service of the Word—the proclamation and faithful hearing of God's Word for us.

The Scriptures form the foundation for everything that is taught and preached in a Christian service.

Since the Holy Spirit creates faith through the Gospel, the congregation responds to the Gospel reading or sermon by confessing the faith in the form of a creed. God has spoken through the Scriptures and the sermon. His Word gives us what it says, and we respond in faith by reciting a common confession of faith.

For many, many centuries, congregations across the

world have used one of the three Ecumenical Creeds on a typical Sunday rather than some sort of statement of faith written specifically for one congregation of a certain denomination. But this isn't a hard and fast rule. Sometimes a hymn might replace the Creed, or in some cases, the congregation confesses the faith using some other words, which can be an acceptable practice as long as those words mean the exact same thing as the ecumenical creeds. But using one of the Ecumenical Creeds shows the unity we claim with the Christian Church through the ages and across the continents. It is one of the ways Christians strive to remember we are called to unity even amid all the divisions among us. We aren't celebrating what makes us different and unique as a congregation, we're celebrating the faith that unites us with our brothers and sisters in Christ. The focus of the creed is on what we have in common, not what is special or different about this particular congregation.

The Service of the Word then ends with the general prayers, which should include everyone the Bible tells Christians to pray for regularly, such as government officials, prisoners, the poor, the work of evangelists, help for those stricken by natural disasters, and so forth, as well as things an individual congregation especially prays for, such as its own local ministries, sick or grieving members, and so on. Additionally, either before or after the prayers, an offering is usually taken. (More about offerings in the next chapter.)

PART 2: **Service of the Sacrament**

It is in the Service of the Sacrament that the worshipers actually receive the true body and blood of Christ in, with, and under bread and wine. Here it is especially important to remember that even though we cannot see it, by faith we know we are entering into the holy place—the throne room of God—when we receive Holy Communion. We are again like Isaiah being taken up into heaven and seeing God. We're helpfully reminded of this fact by the pastor, who concludes the preliminary prayer, or Preface, of the Communion service with the words, "Therefore with angels and archangels and with all the company of heaven we laud and magnify Your glorious name, evermore praising You and saying . . ." (*LSB Altar Book*, p. 161).

> *In the Communion service, we're joining in an already ongoing, eternal, holy song around the throne of God.*

Did you catch that? In the Communion service, we're joining in an already ongoing, eternal, holy song around the throne of God. We aren't starting the song; we're joining "all the company of heaven," which includes those saints who have gone before us. This can be an extremely emotional thing for people grieving the loss of loved ones—for while we are separated for a time in this world, we remain members of the same body and sing together around the same throne.

Picture a huge bonfire with people standing in a large circle around it. If you've ever been a part of such a circle, you know there is an intimacy that comes from singing together even when we can't see everyone who is singing. You can see the people on either side of you, their faces aglow with the fire. But you can't see the people on the other side of the fire. You simply know they are there. That is how it is with our gathering around the throne of the Lamb. We can see the people standing or kneeling on either side of us to receive Communion, but even though we can't see the whole company of heaven, we know by faith that they are there too. It doesn't matter whether the actual church building is a beautiful cathedral or a shabby storefront; by faith, we know that in the Sacrament, the Church, past and present, is united in Christ.

> We can see the people standing or kneeling on either side of us to receive Communion, but even though we can't see the whole company of heaven, we know by faith that they are there too.

And what is the song we sing? It is called the Sanctus (Latin for "holy," which is the first word of the song) and is taken directly from Isaiah, who wrote that all the angels cry out, saying, "Holy, holy, holy Lord God of pow'r and might: Heaven and earth are full of Your glory" (*LSB*, p. 161). This is heavenly worship of Christ.

The next part of the song says, "Hosanna. Hosanna. Hosanna in the highest. Blessed is He who comes in the name of the Lord." These are the words the crowds shouted as Jesus entered into Jerusalem on Palm Sunday, five days before He was crucified. These words represent the earthly worship of Christ. Just as the heavenly song and the earthly song come together to form one song, just as true God and true Man come together in one Christ, so the Church on earth and the Church in heaven come together whenever we gather around the throne of the Lamb and receive the fruit of His victory over sin, death, and hell.

Those liturgical words and songs give us a great context for what is going on, but they themselves are not the Sacrament. The first really indispensable part of the Service of the Sacrament, without which it is no Sacrament, is the Words of Institution. This is where the pastor recites the words Jesus spoke at the Last Supper and consecrates the bread and wine by placing God's Word on them. This consecration is what makes these simple elements into vehicles through which we not only receive bread and wine but also the true body and blood of Christ.

The second crucial, indispensable part of the Sacrament is the distribution of the "elements" (bread and wine) to the worshipers and subsequent consumption of them (not taken home or used in any other way). Different congregations have various ways of distributing the elements. Traditional churches generally have people come forward and kneel or stand at the railing of the chancel in "tables" (the people at the railing with you form your "table"). After everyone has consumed the elements, the people are then dismissed as a table to return to their seats. Depending on the architecture of the building, however, and depending on size, some churches have people form a continuous line and return to their seats as soon as they've received Communion. However it gets done in this or that place, the point remains the same: to distribute Christ's body and blood to the people.

Since the Passover meal calls for unleavened bread, and Passover was what Jesus was celebrating when He instituted Communion, traditional churches often use wafers of unleavened bread to draw the connection between the old covenant and the new, fulfilled-in-Christ covenant. But some churches use a regular loaf of bread, which emphasizes the unity of the congregation—for just as the many grains of wheat came together to make one loaf, so the many congregants partake of the one loaf as at a family meal. Traditionally, the worshipers receive the wafer directly on their tongue, both to emphasize the pure, passive receptivity of the act of taking Communion and also to make sure the people actually eat it. This tradition began back when people were tempted to take the consecrated wafers home to use them for superstitious reasons. Today, even at very traditional churches, the pastor or Communion assistant will be glad to either place the wafer directly onto your tongue or simply place it in your hand, assuming you don't plan on pocketing it as a souvenir.

As for the blood of Christ under the wine (not grape juice, by the way—the biblical word and precedent prescribes wine), traditional churches typically use a "chalice" (fancy cup) from which everyone sips the wine in turn. Since the wine is alcoholic and the chalice is generally coated with a heavy metal, such as silver, and gets wiped after every sip, the common "Eww, that's gross!" reaction is unwarranted. Everyone sipping from the same cup emphasizes the unity of the body. Still, in recent times, many people have objected to sharing a cup for fear of germs, so several churches also offer the option of receiving the blood of Christ in little individual cups.

The idea behind the fancy chalice is that the vessel befit its contents. It is a sacred (not magic, but sacred) thing. That doesn't mean the Sacrament depends on the chalice. It means, for example, that it would be inappropriate (not heretical or illegal, but inappropriate) for someone to drink Diet Coke out of the Communion chalice during the week. The chalice has been set apart for sacred use. Although some people object to its use, saying we shouldn't spend lots of money on a silver- or gold-plated cup, there is a certain confession that comes from the whole congregation sharing the same cup and that cup being gold or silver. Besides the fact that heavy metal is the most sanitary, it symbolizes that no matter how rich you are, the very finest thing you drink out of all week is

You have, and can have, nothing nicer in this world than this Sacrament.

the chalice at church. You have, and can have, nothing nicer in this world than this Sacrament. And no matter how poor you are, the very finest things in the world, like the blood of Christ, are for you too.

After Communion, the congregation often sings the Nunc Dimittis, or Song of Simeon. In Luke 2, Simeon spoke these words after seeing the baby Jesus in the temple. Having received Jesus by faith, we depart in peace with the same wonder and thanksgiving as Simeon when he saw Jesus and knew that God had fulfilled His promise. We receive Jesus by faith, not by sight, and whether we use Simeon's words or some other song of thanksgiving, it is fitting for us to respond just as Simeon did to having God's promises fulfilled in our midst.

The Communion service concludes with the Benediction, or blessing, that the pastor places on the people of God just as God told Aaron to bless His people as they went forth into the Promised Land. The whole liturgy of a traditional worship service consists of verses and concepts straight from the Bible and applies to what is going on in the service at the time. The Song of Simeon applies to coming away from the Communion rail, not to holding the baby Jesus in the temple like Simeon did. And the Benediction is God's blessing to each of us as we go into our separate lives, wherever and however we're living out our baptismal identity as children of God. It is no longer about Aaron and Joshua and all the Israelites, but about the fulfillment of such things in Christ and His people today.

Conclusion

Those twin gifts—the gift of Christ crucified as delivered in the Service of the Word and the gift of Christ crucified and risen as delivered in the Service of the Sacrament—as well as our responses of faith, praise, and prayer, are what worship is all about.

Many people miss these important points and think they are coming to church for inspiration to make it through the week, to get an emotional high, to feel a warm welcome from other people, or to receive practical tips for living the Christian life. Not that inspiration, warmth, emotional highs, and practical tips are

The whole liturgy of a traditional worship service consists of verses and concepts straight from the Bible and applies to what is going on in the service at the time.

bad in themselves, but if we treat them as the main point of worship, then we find ourselves missing out on the greatest blessings that come from participation in worship: Jesus Christ Himself.

CHAPTER 3

MORE THAN "PRAY, PAY, AND OBEY"

Okay, even if the worship service is a great gift to Christians, why does that mean we have to officially join a church? Can't we just attend various churches as we see fit or feel the need rather than sign on the dotted line that makes us formal members?

Whether we use the idea of the family, the flock, or the body, it should be clear that some of the blessings that come from such groupings require knowledge of who is, in fact, a part of the group. The responsibilities of membership have a flip side because each member benefits from the responsibilities of the other members. As a member of the Body of Christ, although you pray for other people; they also pray for you. You aren't the only one sharing your gifts with others; they also share them with you. The responsibilities and benefits of belonging to a church consist of many of the same things flowing back and forth among God's people.

This is especially important when we consider spiritual growth. Spiritual growth hits all kinds of snags, even for the most sanctified of Christians. People's best intentions fall short, and there will always be times when even trying to live a Christian life seems impossible. When you go through such a time, as nearly all Christians do, it really helps to have a mutual sense of accountability within a group of people who won't let you give up or lose your way.

> *Unless you take the plunge and join, you'll always be an observer who never knows the comfort of being part of a family where your place at the table is assured.*

That's what church members have. The perpetual guest, the person who always stands in the doorway listening in, the interested party who likes most of what is going on but who wants to maintain some distance and independence—none of these people ever experience the blessings of really belonging. So unless you take the plunge and join, you'll always be an observer who never knows the comfort of being part of a family where your place at the table is assured, of being part of a flock that has an undershepherd (pastor) of the Good Shepherd, or of being a member of a body that consists of people with very different gifts who use them in concert with yours.

The Church Is Like a Family

Official membership allows a person to live out some aspects of church life that nonmembers typically do not experience. These aspects of church life can sometimes appear to be burdens, which might be why some people prefer not to join a congregation officially. But these burdens often prove to be tremendous blessings in time, and those who turn away from the apparent burden turn away from the less apparent but more important blessings, too. Church life is like family life. What holds people together is not always mutual liking but the fact of the relationship. If you have siblings in a healthy family, you probably can attest that some of the worst spats you've ever had with anyone were with your siblings. But you can probably also attest that among the people you love most and count on the most are your siblings. The bond remains so strong even through those tough times because it was not optional. You could get through the dark tunnels of bad times because you knew you really had no choice; these are your brothers and sisters. And they ultimately prove to be among the greatest blessings in your life precisely because you could not shed the relationship whenever you felt like it.

The people in your congregation can potentially be that kind of blessings to you as well, but it requires some sense of that obligatory, official relationship to get over the inevitable bumps in the road. People you might find annoying until you know what they're going through, people with whom you have little in common and thus wouldn't be likely to get to know, people who are unique and gifted in ways that don't show up in a brief introduction—these are the people who will also be a blessing to you. But if you stay on the periphery and merely participate when you want, you'll find it too easy to gravitate only toward people like yourself. Only when the members do things together and are forced to see one another as family does this breakthrough happen. Talk to someone who has been an active member of a congregation for many years and it is almost guaranteed they will talk about how blessed they are to know people and be built up spiritually by those with whom they otherwise would have had no relationship.

The "Pray" of "Pray, Pay, and Obey"

When it comes to the responsibilities of church membership, you might hear the phrase, "Pray, pay, and obey" as a joke from some long-time faithful churchgoer or as a bitter accusation from a jaded former churchgoer. "All the church wants from me is to pray, pay, and obey," they say. Catchy, isn't it? But is it fair? It has a negative connotation, making it sound as though church members are being used or duped by an organization that simply wants to enrich itself and control people. Like most jokes and accusations, it twists and distorts an element of truth, but it excludes so much and gets so many emphases wrong that it ends up lampooning the truth in an unjust way.

As we saw in the previous chapter, the Church exists to serve, not to be served. Since we are served with such self-sacrificial grace through Word and Sacrament, we naturally want to pass on what we have received.

> *The Church exists to serve, not to be served. Since we are served with such self-sacrificial grace through Word and Sacrament, we naturally want to pass on what we have received.*

ceived. Only by serving its members and the world in this way, in Jesus' name, can a church claim to be the Christian Church that follows Jesus, who said that He came not to be served but to serve. This means that the blessings of church membership do, indeed, come with corresponding responsibilities.

The first of the responsibilities might seem obvious. Woody Allen said 80 percent of success is showing up. People who don't see the blessings of membership tend to be the people who don't show up to church very often. Now, that might seem obvious too. Since they don't see the blessings of membership, they don't show up to church. But the reverse is even more true. Because they don't show up regularly, they don't experience all the blessings. At a practical level, where the rubber hits the road and having certain priorities actually affects your habits and schedules, you have to show up if you want the blessings of being there.

The Third Commandment (Remember the Sabbath day by keeping it holy)—when understood as fulfilled in Christ—is not about a particular day of worship but about receiving Christ, which is what happens in church. About the Third Commandment, Luther's catechism says: "What does this mean? We should fear and love God so that we do not despise preaching and His Word, but hold it sacred and gladly hear and learn it." And here is a typical promise people make when they are received into membership in a congregation: After proclaiming their faith and intention to live as Christians, the prospective new members are asked, "Will you support the work our gracious Lord has given this congregation with your prayers and the gifts God has given you?" They respond with, "We will, with the help of God" (*LSB Agenda*, p. 33). Basically, the members are promising that they will behave like members, which means at the very least showing up for corporate worship on a regular basis and praying for the activities and ministries of the congregation.

The Bible is also quite clear that gathering together for worship is not optional but a key part of being a Christian. "Let us consider how to stir up one another to love and good works, not neglecting to meet together, as is the habit of some, but encouraging one another, and all the more as you see the Day drawing near" (Hebrews 10:24–25). Some of the best ways of stirring up and being stirred up by your fellow Christians is to participate in your congregation's human care ministries.

No congregation can be involved in everything, of course, but every congregation should be closely involved in some kind of special ministry, such as helping to operate a homeless shelter, tutoring struggling children, cleaning up the neighborhood, or a million other possibilities. Whatever your congregation does to help those in need, get involved in that; you will not only be transformed more and more but you will also be God's agent in transforming your fellow church members as they are stirred up to love and good works.

But first things first. More important than any participation in any special congregational causes or programs is participation in the regular Word and Sacrament ministry. Human care ministries are a practical extension of, not a replacement for, worship attendance. Christians are told not to stop meeting together. Apparently some of the earliest Christians, like so many people today, had already begun to make the spiritually deadly mistake of skipping regular worship. They, again like many well-meaning people today, were under the mistaken impression that "going to church" didn't matter for them as long as they had faith. But that misses most of the point about attendance. The key word in the Hebrews passage is "together," which means not only that you benefit from the presence of other people as you sing, pray, and hear the Word, but also that your presence benefits them.

When you decide to skip church, you aren't only deciding for yourself that you can do without Word and Sacrament ministry and the mutual consolation of the brethren for an entire week. You're also unilaterally declaring that everyone else can do just fine without you there. But you are wrong. The indelible impression on young minds of seeing widows and newlyweds, troublemakers and respectable folk, black and white, rich and poor, young and old all singing and praying together can never happen if people don't show up.

When you decide to skip church, you aren't only deciding for yourself that you can do without Word and Sacrament ministry and the mutual consolation of the brethren for an entire week. You're also unilaterally declaring that everyone else can do just fine without you there.

When you stay home because your toddler is too much of a hassle in church, you might be making your morning more manageable, but you're also declaring that the ninety-year-old who sometimes sits behind you will not have your toddler to smile at and thereby have his faith in the future of God's promises reinforced.

Maybe you're an overworked twenty-something who has one day each week to sleep in—and that day is Sunday—and you feel like you don't get much out of church anyway because you already learned it all in Sunday School. When you decide to stay home from church, you get that extra hour of sleep, sure, but you also deprive the twenty-something visitor who is nervous and uncomfortable in church of the assurance your presence gives that says this strange place is a place for them too.

When you as a middle-aged man skip church, you're not only reasoning you have more important places to be, but you are also robbing a fatherless teenage boy whose mom made him go to church that morning of the example your presence in worship might have given.

When you stay home because you're too embarrassed to use the wheelchair, you are robbing your church family of the comfort of seeing that gracefully growing old is possible, and that should the day ever come for them to be in a wheelchair, their church would welcome them as it welcomes you.

No matter who you are or what your situation is, when it says in Hebrews not to stop meeting together, God isn't just telling you that you will be blessed if you go to church. He is also telling you that you are a blessing to others there whether you know it or not. Don't selfishly rob everyone else of the blessing God wants to give them through your voice, your problems, your prayers, and your presence with them in worship.

In addition to what you do when you meet together, there is also the matter of what you do when you are alone. Christians pray. They pray for themselves, for one another, for the ministries of their congregation and church body, and for the world generally. Most congregations print prayer requests in the weekly bulletin that gets handed out in worship. These requests usually include things like members going in for surgery, upcoming mission or service projects, people getting married, grieving the loss of loved ones, and in general all the life situations for which one might want to be prayed. Some congregations have prayer circles or email chains that announce prayer requests to members. An amazing number of people take the bulletin home and use the list of prayer requests every day in their personal devotions. So even if you only actually get together on Sunday, you might have people praying for you on Tuesday morning as you go in for a job interview or have medical tests done. What a blessing! And, of course, when you have the bulletin yourself (or email or whatever your congregation provides to people), you have the same opportunity to pray during the week for those with whom you worshiped and communed on Sunday, specific people with specific needs in your congregation. And, of course, every specific thing on your congregation's calendar that week—a youth service project, a neighborhood outreach event, a meeting of a cancer survivor's support group—needs the prayers of the members. By praying and being prayed for during the week, you are blessed by God through others, and you are a blessing from God to others.

So in the snide little "Pray, pay, and obey" slogan, prayer refers to attending worship, praying for and participating in the congregation's ministries, and keeping the congregation, its pastor, the other members, and the ministries in your personal prayers. All of those things are perfectly legitimate, good, and necessary things for Christians to do as we stir one another up to love and good works.

The "Pay" of "Pray, Pay, and Obey"

But what about "pay?" Money and the church tends to be a toxic combination for many church members. And rightfully so, in many cases. Too many people have been taken in by hucksters and profiteers, wolves in sheep's clothing, who present themselves as preachers and end up getting rich. Once bitten, twice shy, as they say. There are indeed a lot of false preachers and teachers out there, and some churches and ministries do indeed have an unhealthy interest in acquiring wealth.

The Scriptures are clear about "mammon," or "filthy lucre," that is, money and worldly goods: the love and pursuit of such things are spiritual poison. Jesus goes so far as to say that you cannot love both God and

If you join a church where the preacher rarely touches on any topic that makes you uncomfortable, you probably have a bad case of IES–Itching Ears Syndrome.

money. In the parable of the sower (Matthew 13), Jesus says the "deceitfulness of riches" (v. 22) is one of the weeds that chokes the Gospel's chance to bear fruit in our lives.

For this reason, if a preacher wants to be faithful, he has no choice but to warn his church members about this danger. Thus, money is bound to come up on a fairly regular basis in sermons and Bible studies, and the church members need to listen with an open ear for what God is saying in His Word about the insidious role the love of money can play in our spiritual lives. And it will likely make people uncomfortable. It is supposed to.

If you join a church where the preacher rarely touches on any topic that makes you uncomfortable, you probably have a bad case of IES—Itching Ears Syndrome. That term comes from St. Paul's Letter to Timothy, in which he instructed Timothy on how to be a Christian pastor. In that letter, Paul writes,

> I charge you [Timothy, but by extension all pastors] in the presence of God and of Christ Jesus, who is to judge the living and the dead, and by His appearing and His kingdom: preach the word; be ready in season and out of season; reprove, rebuke, and exhort, with complete patience and teaching. For the time is coming when people will not endure sound teaching, but having itching ears they will accumulate for themselves teachers to suit their own passions. (2 Timothy 4:1–3)

The meaning is fairly clear—we prefer preachers who tell us what we want to hear, what our ears itch to hear, especially when it comes to money. Our natural passions, ambitions, and appetites, which are warped by sin, don't want to be rebuked. They want to be endorsed, excused, or at the very least ignored.

Left untreated, Itching Ears Syndrome is spiritually fatal. Of course, it applies to more than just money issues. It could be sexual morality, respect for authorities, or any number of other aspects of life. But with the possible exception of the desire to have one's sexual sins legitimated and called good or acceptable, the desire to keep the church out of one's wallet, to complain that the church is only interested in money, is the biggest symptom of IES. So pastors know they cannot simply decide to never talk about money in their sermons. They have to talk about it in order to be faithful shepherds. The "cure of souls" they engage in has to address the disease, and in the case of Itching Ears Syndrome and the topic of money, the medicine tastes terrible at first. But getting healthy feels better and better, and mature Christians, whether rich or poor, often speak of opportunities to contribute and support the missions of the Church as one of the greatest blessings in life. We can all hear the words, "It is more blessed to give than to receive" (Acts 20:35), but learning the truth of those words takes a long time, and the first steps down that road are often the most painful.

When it comes to the "pay" part of "Pray, pay and obey," most Christians speak in terms of "tithing," or offering the "firstfruits" of what God has given us. This is the biblical example that goes all the way back to Genesis 4 when Abel offered God the best of his flock, and also, perhaps especially, to later in Genesis when Abraham gave Melchizedek, the priest of God Most High, a tenth of everything as an offering. You can read about the significance of this in the seventh chapter of the Book of Hebrews. The point here is that such tithes and offerings have a long and established pedigree as the sound practice of the people of God. A tithe is a tenth, that is, ten percent of one's income. In addition to the ancient precedent of it, there are several theological and practical reasons why tithing is a good practice for Christians today.

Theologically, tithing helps us understand our lives as a matter of stewardship and realize the thanks we ought to give for all God's gifts in our lives. It also encourages us to learn more and more to walk by faith. Tithing is our way of recognizing that all we have comes from God. One famous hymn puts it this way: "We give Thee but Thine own, Whate'er the gift may be; All that we have is Thine alone, A trust, O Lord, from Thee" (*LSB* 781). What that hymn says is that we are stewards or managers, not owners, of all that we have. Furthermore, when we acknowledge the fact that everything we have is a gift from God, we naturally offer thanks, and we express that gratitude in part via tithing. Of course we cannot say thank you to God by giving Him anything that wasn't already His to begin with, but we dedicate back to God's service the firstfruits as the symbolic representative of the whole of our lives.

Tithing also expresses faith in God's "providence," that is, trust that God will always provide. Let's face it, at first, ten percent seems like an awful lot of money. Most new church members naturally assume they can't afford to tithe. After all, it isn't like they've been wondering what to do with all the extra money lying around

Tithing helps us learn to trust, to go by faith rather than by sight.

at the end of the month. But that's part of the point. Tithing helps us learn to trust, to go by faith rather than by sight. If you go by sight, you'll quickly conclude that tithing is impossible—at least for you. But then you meet people who do it and find out they are like you. Only the actual witness of the many tithers in the congregation convinces us that it is far more doable than we think, and doing it is a far greater blessing than we can conceive until we start trying to do it.

At a practical level, there are several things to consider about your offerings.

- "God loves a cheerful giver." Offering expresses what is in your heart or, on your bad days, what you know ought to be in your heart. Tithing isn't a law. Nowhere does the Bible say you can't be a Christian unless you tithe. If it did, people would tithe out of a sense of self-righteousness as though doing so made them good enough or otherwise earned them a relationship with God. Tithing is supposed to be a response to God's free gifts and therefore like God's free gifts, not something you owe but something you give despite not owing it, just like God does. Tithing is such a good practice that sometimes people recommending it make it seem as though it is a law, which is a mistake. It is just that some people can't even get started working toward tithing unless they think of it as a law.

- God doesn't need your money. In fact, He doesn't need anything from you. Tithes and offerings are for your sake; they do you spiritual good. They also serve your neighbor. A self-righteousness creeps in when we think we're doing God a favor by contributing to the church.

- Your tithes and offerings are a gift, not a loan or an investment. That means it isn't your money anymore once you've offered it. If you make your offerings conditional on how the money is spent, you're trying to control something that is no longer yours, which means you aren't really giving it up at all. It is an act of trust in and solidarity with your brothers and sisters in Christ that you can rely on one another to support the ministries of the congregation and larger church body even though everyone has their own ideas of how the money should be spent and nobody fully gets their way. If you really want to support specific missions and ministries that your congregation doesn't include in its budget, you should resist the temptation to redirect the tithes that would normally go to the congregation. Those donations to specific things you favor should be over and above your regular tithes and offerings.

- Some necessary things are boring. The key is to understand everything at church in ministry terms. Yes, everyone likes to see their money go toward funding some dramatic cause, but even contributions to emergency relief efforts go in part toward things like gas and vehicle maintenance on supply trucks, postage and printing costs for the flyers calling for contributions, and all kinds of fixed overhead costs. We like to think of it as "help for earthquake victims," which is dramatic, and we accept that what that looks like in reality is far more mundane. Your congregation is the same way. If you're going to have a church to go to, it needs a new furnace every twenty years or so. It needs to pay the electric bills, the copier repair company, and all kinds of costs. Nobody rallies around such mundane costs, because they're boring. It helps to remember what all those boring bills are in reality—an outpost of the kingdom of God offering Word and Sacrament ministry to His people and in need of equipment and manpower to serve effectively.

- Your pastor and other full-time servants of the church deserve a decent living. This is not an optional thing, it is a biblical rule. "In the same way, the Lord commanded that those who proclaim the gospel should get their living by the gospel" (1 Corinthians 9:14). St. Paul offered himself as an exception to his own rule. He realized it is an awkward thing to realize that the pastor's livelihood ultimately comes out of the offering plate. There is an old joke that says everyone wants the pastor to have a nice family, but nobody wants to pay to put his kids through school. That attitude doesn't work. While what constitutes enough to "make a living" differs from place to place, common sense says that whatever salary the phrase implies in the minds of the parishioners when thinking of themselves should also apply when they think of their pastor. If the average parishioner wouldn't consider a certain amount to be properly "making a living" for himself, then he should not expect his pastor to make a living on that amount either. That is just simple fairness and the meaning of loving your neighbor as yourself. By the same token, the pastor must be content and not use his position to enrich himself or focus on the worldly comfort and benefits that come from a generous salary. Multiple times the Bible says that preachers and teachers must not be lovers of money. There can be faithful congregations that are simply unable to pay a pastor much of a salary, and there can be pastors like St. Paul who are willing and able to work without being paid. But a pastor who is all about his salary is not a good pastor, and a congregation that refuses to pay its pastor enough to make a living despite having the wherewithal to do so is not a faithful congregation.

- When you put money in the offering plate, you are trusting your brothers and sisters in Christ to make good decisions with it. They're putting the same trust in you. Once a year, your congregation will probably have a budget meeting, and like most budget meetings, it is likely to be boring. Go to it anyway. Bring ideas. Bring a genuinely open mind toward other people's ideas. Participate. Remember, you aren't just looking at a bunch of tedious line items in the proposed budget. You're looking at what it takes to equip and staff an outpost of the Church Militant, the kingdom of heaven on earth.

The "Obey" of "Pray, Pay, and Obey"

Probably no word or idea has a worse reputation than obedience. People naturally hate the idea. It seems belittling, infantilizing even, to have to obey someone. Yet everyone likes to give orders and be obeyed. This makes obedience a particularly difficult concept for Christians who know we are all sinners. Obedience is one of the most important and most dangerous things in human society. On one hand, we have to resist our own natural, sinful resistance to obeying. On the other hand, we have to remain vigilant toward anyone demanding to be obeyed, testing them against God's Word. Being in charge is a sacred trust, one that is very easy to betray.

Obedience is one of the most important and most dangerous things in human society.

Consider what St. Paul says to church members about how to follow their leaders:

> Remember your leaders, those who spoke to you the word of God. Consider the outcome of their way of life,

and imitate their faith. . . . Obey your leaders and submit to them, for they are keeping watch over your souls, as those who will have to give an account. Let them do this with joy and not with groaning, for that would be of no advantage to you. (Hebrews 13:7, 17)

The key is that they not only speak the Word of God but also seek (imperfectly, because they're sinners too) to model what it means to live according to the Word of God. There may be areas of your life that you regard as absolutely none of anyone else's business. However, you are called as a Christian to conform to the Word of God, and in such matters you might be deviating from sound, biblical teaching. Your pastor is the one God has placed in your life to call you back, to remind you, and in some cases insist that you change your ways. That is his job. And it is your job to listen.

> Your pastor is the one God has placed in your life to call you back, to remind you, and in some cases insist that you change your ways. That is his job. And it is your job to listen.

Crucially, however, obedience to your pastor does not mean he gets to boss you around. It means he must apply God's Word to you, both Law and Gospel. You aren't called to obey your pastor personally, but God working through your pastor. When you listen to

God's Word applied to you through the pastor, you are really obeying God. Your pastor can't order you to take this or that job, select this or that doctor, buy this or that car or house or anything like that. That isn't the kind of authority he has.

Since there is no scriptural basis or command from God at stake, those things really are none of your pastor's business. But some things *are* his business. Where Christian doctrine speaks to your choices, your pastor must speak. It is his business to do so.

You aren't called to obey your pastor personally, but God working through your pastor.

Consider a few examples. Say your marriage is crumbling. You don't know what to do and are considering filing for divorce. Your Lord and Savior has some things to say about that topic. Therefore, His representative in your life, your pastor, has things he must say about the topic, and he must insist you listen. But it is intimately your own personal, private decision, right? Wrong. Sadly, pastors often find out about struggling marriages only after one or both spouses have already decided to get a divorce. That is backward. The pastor is supposed to be part of the decision, or, hopefully, part of the solution to the problems that led up to it even being an issue in the first place. Of course, a particular pastor does not have this God-given task in everyone's life. He has this role only in the lives of his flock, the members of his congregation.

This is another important reason to make your membership in the Body of Christ concrete in the form of membership in a congregation.

The same idea applies to the beginning of marriages too. Society differs greatly from the norms of sound Christian teaching in some areas, probably none greater than the question of premarital sex and cohabitation. The world says it is fine, or at least that it's no biggie. Christianity has always said, No, it is not fine. Your pastor teaches and preaches about this sometimes. He should not be the last one to find out you're living with your boyfriend or girlfriend. You might find yourself in the position of having to obey his application of God's Word despite your own wishes on the matter.

Dealing with an unwanted pregnancy is another major example. God's Word has many things to say about how we are to deal with such matters. For Christians, an unplanned pregnancy is not a personal, private matter. "But, but, but . . ." some might object, "all those examples relate to sex somehow. Why is the Church so obsessed with sex?" The Church, which lives in a sex-obsessed culture, seeks to apply God's Word. Sex, like money, is an area of life about which people naturally feel very private and suspicious of anyone else expressing an opinion. But your pastor isn't called to offer his opinion. He will, probably, if asked, but his opinion isn't the point. God's Word is. Every Christian deep down knows that.

The "obey" aspect of the faith shows up most clearly in those areas of our lives we consider the most personal and private and in which the Church's teachings contradict the world's—and maybe even our own—expectations most directly. That means money and sex tend to be the two headline-grabbing topics. On the topic of money, as we've seen, each member has to remain vigilant, because the church, being comprised of sinners, also can be subject to ulterior motives when asking for or demanding money. Not so with sex. The church and your pastor get no benefit for themselves by calling people to live a certain way in terms of how they use their bodies. God has simply called pastors to "reprove, rebuke, and exhort" the flock, and in this case train people up with the knowledge that "You are not your own, for you were bought with a price. So honor God in your body" (2 Corinthians 6:19–20). This is not your pastor's opinion, nor does it reflect mere meddling in your life. God indeed calls you, for your own good, to obey His Word and the pastors who teach it faithfully. Even when obedience promises difficulty, we remember that the Christ we Christians follow was first and foremost "obedient" even unto death. And we who would call ourselves His followers must not think of obedience, even difficult obedience, as superfluous to the act of following Him.

Conclusion

So "Pray, pay, and obey," can come across as a snide description of the Church's self-serving teachings, but when we look more closely at the realities of church life, we find that some reasons people have for refusing to join a church are actually good reasons to join, and things most people naturally dislike or think too difficult, like tithing or being corrected, would actually be big blessings to them if they understood them in light of God's Word.

CHAPTER 4

"TRUST, BUT VERIFY"

When Ronald Reagan famously said these words, he was talking about nuclear arms reduction pacts, but the saying also applies to the trust we place in our fallen, sinful pastors and congregations.

If you or someone you know has ever had cancer, you've probably dealt firsthand with chemotherapy. Essentially, chemotherapy works like deliberate poisoning. Depending on the type of cancer and the treatment, chemotherapy can devastate a person's whole body in an effort to kill the cancer cells. Very few cancer patients understand which chemicals to apply, how much and how often, how to counteract the terrible side effects, and so forth. Most patients do not hold a doctorate degree in biochemistry. They have to trust their doctors. So they often also verify. They research everything they can about their kind of cancer. They inquire about their doctor's reputation in the field. They pepper their doctor with questions. If they're going to entrust their very lives to this person, they want to make sure that this person knows what he or she is doing.

The same principle applies to a lesser degree to the trust we have in our legal representatives, financial advisors, mechanics, electricians, and plumbers. We "trust, but verify." In most cases, we have no choice but to trust; after all, they know how to do their job and we don't. But because dishonest mechanics, incompetent doctors, corrupt lawyers, and so forth do indeed exist in this fallen world, we have a responsibility in so far as we are able to hold them to the standards of their trade.

Pastors and congregations are no different. We discussed previously that a congregation's confession, creedal statements, or statement of faith is really the most important thing about it. The content of the preaching and teaching focused on Christ is "the faith" being handed down from the apostles. Therefore, the Christian faith as confessed is what unites the members to the congregation and the congregation to the Body of Christ, and thereby to Christ Himself, the Head of the Body. When the preaching and teaching errs, it leads people astray and into spiritual danger. So just as you "trust, but verify" when it comes to the doctor to whom you're entrusting your life, so should you do with the pastor and congregation to which you are, in a sense, entrusting your spiritual life, the health of your soul.

Anyone can read the congregation's confessional statements that detail what exactly the congregation believes, teaches, and confesses. So checking up on that, although sometimes challenging, is pretty straightforward. The congregation will probably give you a copy when, or before, you join. On rare but dangerous occasions, however, a pastor or influential layperson might contradict the congregation's confession of faith, perhaps in sermons or Bible studies. This deviation from sound teaching can go in all kinds of different directions for all kinds of reasons, but the point is that the members of the congregation must be ready to admonish even their pastors or influential members to ensure that their teaching and preaching conforms to the sound confession of faith.

When a pastor is "installed" (yes, it sounds like putting in a new furnace, but that is the term for it) in a congregation and officially becomes its pastor, he makes various promises. The wording might not always be the exact same in every case, but at some point, the pastor confesses his personal faith/belief in the congregation's confession of faith and promises to preach and teach according to it. At a Lutheran church, the questions asked of the pastor might sound something like this:

> Do you believe and confess the canonical books of the Old and New Testaments to be the Inspired Word of God and the only infallible rule of faith and practice?

Do you believe and confess the three Ecumenical Creeds, namely, the Apostles', the Nicene, and the Athanasian Creeds, as faithful testimonies to the truth of the Holy Scriptures, and do you reject all the errors which they condemn?

Do you confess the Unaltered Augsburg Confession to be a true exposition of Holy Scripture and a correct exhibition of the doctrine of the Evangelical Lutheran Church? And do you confess [the rest of the confession documents in the Book of Concord] are also in agreement with this one scriptural faith?

Do you promise that you will perform the duties of your office in accordance with these Confessions, and that all your preaching and teaching and your administration of the Sacraments will be in conformity with the Holy Scripture and with these Confessions? (*LSB Agenda*, 165–66)

The pastor says yes to all the questions, and the congregation in turn promises to receive him as their pastor with all the support and obedience that entails. But what if the pastor fails to live up to his promises? The whole congregation has a responsibility to not only keep its own promises to the pastor but also to make sure the pastor lives up to the promises he made to all the members.

The role of pastor differs from the role of a doctor or mechanic in many ways, but in one way in particular. In most cases, you can "fire" anyone you hire. (The customer is always right, as they say.) But because pastors are called by God to address the old Itching Ears Syndrome, they are, by God's design, an exception to this rule. God calls your pastor to your congregation through the voters' assembly. Your congregation does not "hire" the pastor, nor can they fire him. If it worked like that (and sadly in some places, it does—with bad consequences in the long run), then the itchy-eared folks would always get their way and the service of the pastor would become counterproductive to its purpose. Those needing correction would instead find encouragement for their errors and habitual sins.

But because pastors, too, are sinners, situations sometimes arise in which the members of the congregation must remove their pastor from office. Those situations include instances in which the pastor simply can no longer carry out his duties, perhaps due to mental or physical health problems; or the pastor's life becomes a cause for public scandal, say, because he cheated on his wife, embezzled funds, or otherwise grossly and publicly failed in his duty to adorn the office with a holy life; or the pastor publicly preached or taught contrary to the confession of faith to which he promised to adhere. Any of those situations might be grounds for removing the pastor. But it's important to remember that not liking him personally is not on the list.

The person or personality of the pastor often takes on way too much importance in people's minds. People naturally gravitate toward charismatic personalities, lively and funny sermons, warm hugs, firm handshakes, and all kinds of perfectly innocent things that have little to do with the gifts God gives through the pastor. Yet in a way, it is the pastor's job, especially in the service itself, to match the furniture, so to speak. What does that mean? Every way in which God distributes His grace and forgiveness in worship typically has a piece of furniture associated with it—usually an altar where God gives the gift of Christ's body and blood, a baptismal font where He adopts people via Baptism into His family and declares them His children, a lectern where God's Word is publicly read from the Bible, and a pulpit where the Law and the Gospel are proclaimed to the people. In some places, those pieces of furniture are beautiful and ornate. In others, they are quite plain and simple. In many churches, those special furnishings associated with the Word and Sacraments get decorated with matching "paraments," which are colored fabrics that go along with the seasons of the Church Year. And generally, those paraments also match the "stole," the band of fabric draped over the pastor's shoulders signifying that he is the pastor in that place. The pastor, like those pieces of furniture, is an instrument of God's grace. It is really nice to have a pastor you like, someone with whom you have a personal connection. But it isn't necessary to what happens in church.

In the same way, it is really nice to have a beautiful baptismal font or an impressive altar. But they don't need to be beautiful in order to fulfill their function. As long as you have water and the Word, there can be a glorious Baptism, even if the font containing the water is ugly. And as long as you have a called and ordained servant of the Word announcing forgiveness and proclaiming the Good News, it really doesn't matter that much whether you find it easy to get along with him. He is there to provide a specific set of gifts and serve a specific function. He is there, figuratively speaking, to match the furniture, sometimes by literally wearing a piece of clothing that matches the clothing draped on the other furnishings set apart for the delivery of God's gifts. It isn't the appeal of the furniture but their function in bringing the gifts of God's grace in Word and Sacrament that matter. It isn't the personality of the pastor that really matters but his official role and function as the one who delivers God's gifts. If you have them, be thankful for a beautiful altar and a pastor you like personally. But don't confuse the beauty of the altar with the importance of what rests upon it, and don't confuse your friendship with the pastor with the importance of what he is there to give you.

To be sure, the pastor's ability to connect with you does matter to some degree. When it comes to counseling, teaching, or being a role model, he will always serve more effectively with a winsome personality and good people skills. But no one can connect with everyone. In every congregation, there will be people who truly get along well with the pastor and others who merely tolerate him at a personal level. You might be one of the former or the latter, and it is okay either way.

A further responsibility every Christian has toward the congregation involves how to handle gossip, complaints, and members' sins against one another. Matthew 18 outlines a specific process for resolving disputes. Additionally, the Eighth Commandment demands that we not engage in gossip or slander but explain everything in the kindest way, especially when the person being talked about is absent. Too often everyone gets along just fine in a meeting or while shaking hands after church, but out in the parking lot or over lunch, the knives come out and the organist, pastor, or other church leader becomes the topic of conversation—their reputations shredded by people who don't like how they do things. This kind of conversation poisons the fellowship. Every member must be on guard and not only refuse to listen but also seek to defend the person being so slandered. You wouldn't think this would be a problem among Christians, but it is and always will be as long as Christians are sinners.

Conclusion

"Trust, but verify" not only means holding your pastor accountable; it means holding your fellow church members accountable and, in turn, being willing to let them hold you accountable. In this way, the blessings and responsibilities of church membership merge into one relationship held together by mutual faith in Christ and trust in one another. You, your fellow church members, and your pastor(s) all share a confession of faith. You trust one another to uphold it, but you should also verify, that is, regularly check to make sure that everything your pastor and congregation proclaim and do aligns with that confession of faith.

CHAPTER 5

RESPONDING TO OBJECTIONS TO CHURCH MEMBERSHIP

There is an old joke made famous by Groucho Marx that you've probably heard some variation of. It goes something like, "I wouldn't join any club that would have someone like me as a member." The joke, of course, is in the contradiction. Marx is claiming that he himself is too good to be associated with bad people like himself, which obviously makes no sense. But it is funny, because it strikes a nerve. People really do think that way.

The Church Is Too Hypocritical and Too Judgmental

You see this contradictory line of thinking in the two biggest complaints about the church you'll likely hear from people who have either left the church or refused to ever consider joining in the first place: "They're a bunch of hypocrites" and "They're so judgmental."

The complaint that the Church is full of hypocrites is completely true when looked at from one perspective. Hypocrites are two-faced people, those who lead double lives, who do the things they condemn or fail to do the things they say are important to do. Since Christians are sinners called to holiness, the things we aspire to, the things we say are good, will not always show up in what we do. As St. Paul says in Romans 7, "For I do not understand my own actions. For I do not do what I want, but I do the very thing that I hate. . . . For I have the desire to do what is right, but not the ability to carry it out. For I do not do the good I want, but the evil I do not want is what I keep on doing" (vv. 15, 18b–19). But what is an internal spiritual struggle for St. Paul might look to an outsider like mere hypocrisy. St. Paul condemns something, and then he does it himself. That's all an outsider would see. So a Christian struggling with his or her own sinful nature appears to an outsider like someone who doesn't walk the talk. We Christians know we can't perfectly walk the talk. That's why we gather around forgiveness first and foremost.

People also often condemn the Church for being too judgmental. The Church, it seems to them, is always condemning, always pointing out sins, always telling people they aren't good enough. Such people think of Christianity as a set of rules to live by; they think Christians aren't allowed to do anything fun and that they look down on those who do have fun. Or they think Christians look down on those who have made big mistakes in life, as though they are better than such people. No one wants to feel judged and condemned. And of course, Jesus tells us not to judge. But Jesus does indeed judge. That's part of who He is. He condemns sin on the road to forgiving it, calling people to repent of their sins. And since the proclamation of God's harsh, accusatory Law appears in every church service, everyone ought to come away feeling or knowing that they are sinners. Christians who know forgiveness sometimes forget that some outsiders only know the accusation part. That's

We Christians know we can't perfectly walk the talk. That's why we gather around forgiveness first and foremost.

what stands out to them. Every Christian must be on guard against people's tendency to think that way and help the whole congregation make sure that the main impression of the Church and Christian life, especially to outsiders, is one of Christ and His forgiveness.

But look at the no-win situation in which that puts a typical congregation. Say someone who really struggles with some obvious sins wants to join your church. Maybe it is even someone just like St. Paul. If the congregation says, "Great, you're in. Welcome aboard," then that person with all his or her public and obvious sins is out there all week representing your congregation as a member. People will look at that person and naturally think, "Yeah, those people in that congregation talk a good game on Sunday, but look at them the rest of the week. What a bunch of hypocrites!" But if the congregation insists this person amend his or her life first in order to better reflect sound Christian teaching, then people will naturally say, "They say they're all about grace and forgiveness, but really they're just about condemning people. They're so judgmental."

Every person who joins a church is a sinner. They represent the congregation and the Church wherever they go. The person who stays away from church either because Christians are hypocrites or because they're so judgmental is trying to say, "I wouldn't join a church that would have me as a member."

So what can the members of the congregation do to counteract this catch-22 of being either hypocritical or judgmental? First, work to minimize the truth of the accusation. Yes, the accusation is not necessarily fair or to the point, but it probably hurts because it hits close to home. We really are sinners who fail, and outsiders see that. We need to remember how important it is to walk the talk, and how much it hurts the Church's witness to the world when we fail. We need to realize how easy it is to fall into the temptation of judging everyone all the time and coming across as holier-than-thou to outsiders. Those are real problems. But the solution to them is also real. We focus on grace and forgiveness, modeling not a moral perfection that is beyond our grasp but the repentance and faith in Christ that we have been given and that comforts repentant sinners.

In the end, we cannot expect to argue, convince, or otherwise overcome by our own powers the very real objections outsiders raise about the Church. We know that what we preach and teach is foolishness to the world and a stumbling block (see 1 Corinthians 1:23). We can hardly complain when they treat the Church as though it is exactly what they see. Only the Holy Spirit can convert hearts. So, rather than getting defensive when people attack us as foolish, hypocritical, and judgmental,

> *Rather than getting defensive when people attack us as foolish, hypocritical, and judgmental, we should seek to offer the Gospel to those people in the hopes that the Holy Spirit will open their eyes to the deeper truth and give them faith in Christ too.*

which is exactly what we are apart from Christ and exactly what we look like to anyone who lacks the eyes of faith in Christ, we should seek to offer the Gospel to those people in the hopes that the Holy Spirit will open their eyes to the deeper truth and give them faith in Christ too.

The Church Isn't Anything Like it Should Be

Another common objection to church membership often comes from committed readers of the Bible who want personal faith without some sort of official institution and membership roster. What they point out is that the Book of Acts seems to describe a church that is quite different from the typical congregation today. Take a look, for example, at the description of the earliest believers.

> And they devoted themselves to the apostles' teaching and the fellowship, to the breaking of bread and the prayers. And awe came upon every soul, and many wonders and signs were being done through the apostles. And all who believed were together and had all things in common. And they were selling their possessions and belongings and distributing the proceeds to all, as any had need. And day by day, attending the temple together and breaking bread in their homes, they received their food with glad and generous hearts, praising God and favor with all the people. And the Lord added to their number day by day those who were being saved. (Acts 2:42–47)

At first blush, if you look only at these verses, the Early Church indeed seems to be some sort of commune. Very few, if any, modern churches look like what these verses describe, so it appears that the criticism is valid. Never mind that the one making the criticism probably wouldn't join the church even if it did look like the church of the early chapters of Acts. Why don't today's churches act like those in the Early Church? The surprising answer is that, in fact, most churches do. The astonishing thing that shines through when you take time to look is that despite all the vast changes in the world over the last two thousand years, people all over the world are still doing exactly what those first Christians did. Sure, it looks a little different, but the continuity is clear. As a massive oak tree is to an acorn or little sapling, so is the Church of today to the group of believers in Acts.

Look at what being a follower of Jesus means. It means the same for you as it did for the Early Church. They devoted themselves to the apostles' teaching. That's why your church should be first and foremost defined by its confession of faith, making clear that it is biblical and in continuity with the apostles and the Church through the ages. The Lutheran Confessions, for example, make clear that a Lutheran church is supposed to believe, teach, and confess the apostles' teaching—and no novelty introduced in the intervening years. To be a follower of Jesus like the people in Acts 2 means to care deeply about doctrine and to devote oneself to learning it and living by it.

What else do followers of Jesus devote themselves to? The fellowship. Again, they understood themselves as members, not individuals, with a relationship to Jesus. Think about that phrase "devoted to the fellowship." You can hardly say you're rejecting membership in the church, which is simply another word for the fellowship, based on the example of the earliest Christians; they devoted themselves to the fellowship. They belonged to it and it to them. Simply being a participating member is the very least one can do if one wants to devote oneself to the fellowship like the people in Acts 2 did.

What else did the earliest followers of Jesus devote themselves to? Going to church. Sure, they referred to it as breaking of bread and the prayers, but if you think about it, if you go to a church service today (which, again, is actually two services in one—the service of the Word and the service of the Sacrament) almost the whole thing will consist of the proclaiming of the apostles' teaching, the breaking of bread in Holy Communion, and prayers. In fact, someone who really wants their church to be like the church in Acts should be insisting that the services be offered more frequently than just on Sunday.

As a massive oak tree is to an acorn or little sapling, so is the Church of today to the group of believers in Acts.

Now, obviously the actual apostles are all dead and awaiting the very resurrection they taught the Church about all those years ago, so we don't have the same signs and wonders today that God did through them. But those signs and wonders were necessary back then in order to establish the first community of believers. Jesus even told the apostles themselves that they got to see and believe, but blessed would be those who followed them who would not see and yet believe (see John 20:29). We have the New Testament in written form, which the earliest Christians didn't have. St. John, the apostle who survived the longest, wrote in his Gospel, "Now Jesus did many other signs in the presence of the disciples, which are not written in this book; but these are written so that you may believe that Jesus is the Christ, the Son of God, and that by believing you may have life in His name" (John 20:30–31). Amazingly, this means that **you** are mentioned in the Bible. "You" refers to the reader. St. John can't show you signs and wonders anymore, but he did bequeath to you his testimony of Jesus Christ, and the Holy Spirit normally uses that, rather than signs and wonders, to bring people to faith and membership in the ever-growing fellowship of the Church today.

The description of the earliest church goes on to talk about how the believers were selling their possessions, giving to those in need, and having everything in common. One thing to realize is that as the Church grew, even in the Book of Acts and in St. Paul's letters, it is clear that Christians did not abandon the idea of private property. St. Paul tells people who were abusing the Communion service to eat meals at home so as to be able to focus on the sacramental nature of Holy Communion rather than taking Communion because they were physically hungry (1 Corinthians 11:20–34). He also tells people to earn their own living if at all possible (2 Thessalonians 3:12). And notice that they broke bread in their homes, which they couldn't have done if they'd all sold their homes. No, the two things at issue here are common ownership of the things pertaining to the fellowship and a dedication to serving the poor.

Let's look at those two facets. First, common ownership. Go into any church, preferably a nice, substantial looking one. Now ask yourself, who owns this? Whose silver chalice is that? Whose beautiful stained glass windows? Whose acreage? The answer is that everything pertaining to the fellowship is still owned in common. Sure, in some places there are little commemorations of who donated various items, but who donated them is not the same thing as who owns them. If you join a church, then before you've contributed a dime to it, that church is every bit as much yours as anyone else's. Even people who've been tithing to that church for decades and have donated hundreds of thousands of dollars to its ministries do not own it more than you do once you join. Many churches have buildings and grounds worth millions of dollars; what an incredible thing that they're owned in common. The poor as well as the rich can walk into their church and say, "This is mine because I belong to the fellowship."

Christian churches also devote themselves to those in need. This effort takes a variety of forms. First, there is the issue of need among the members of the fellowship. Nearly every church will do whatever it takes to help its members who are poverty-stricken. They do not generally advertise this, because it is easy to abuse. St. Paul says, when speaking of members of the fellowship, that anyone who refuses to work should not eat (2 Thessalonians 3:10). The design is not for people to join the Church just to get someone else to pay their bills. But if you are an active member of the Church and you lose everything in a house fire, or you have exorbitant medical bills, or you lose your job and now they're threatening to cut off your electricity, talk to the pastor. Almost assuredly, your church will help in some way, perhaps with a benefit dinner, a special offering, or something else. In many churches, wealthier members often give over and above their normal tithes to a special fund and ask their pastors that it be designated to help members of the fellowship who have genuine physical needs. And, in my experience, these generous people often give anonymously, so as not to be thanked or rewarded. Again, because this is so easy to abuse and all Christians are sinners, it is important to remember that receiving money from the church is not supposed to be a regular occurrence or a way of life. Nor is it something people should seek simply to remain comfortable; it is supposed to help with genuine physical needs, not mere desires. But even then, in most congregations, people who can't afford niceties like a special Thanksgiving dinner or Christmas presents for their family can probably count on their church for some assistance if the need is real and fellow church members have the wherewithal to help.

As for those outside the fellowship, typically churches do not simply hand out money to strangers. They'll operate or contribute to a food pantry or shelter, and sometimes in emergencies will offer bus passes or a gas card. The reason churches don't just hand out cash is not because they don't want to be generous; it is because they want to *help* those in need, and handing out money with no strings attached isn't necessarily the best way to do so (not to mention the fact that most churches are not awash with unlimited cash).

On a larger scale, if you took away all the hospitals, orphanages, schools, crisis pregnancy centers, homeless shelters, and other places that serve the neediest among us that were founded and/or operated by Christians, there'd be precious few left. Most congregations can't operate a large-scale operation on their own, but they pitch in and, through their denomination, help to run such entities. And on a more local scale, where do Alcoholics Anonymous and related groups that help people deal with addiction go when they need a place to meet? Churches. Where do volunteers teach English to immigrants? Who donates the diapers, formula, and other critical supplies to pro-life pregnancy counseling centers? Churches.

Most churches, held in common by all the members of the fellowship, do indeed give to any as have need to the best of their abilities. They can always do more and better, but they won't ever be able to do that if their own members don't stir one another up to good works because they can't even be bothered to become members at all.

"And the Lord added to their number day by day those who were being saved" (Acts 2:47b). They numbered about 120 in Acts 1 (how did they know whom to count and whom not to count if they didn't have "members" back then?) and they were still a small band in Acts 2, but a lot of "day by day" has happened since then, and currently the Christians in the world number in the billions. Sure, some congregations struggle and lose members, and Christianity seems to wane in some areas. But globally, Christianity marches on as it ever has, the living continuation of the Acts of the Apostles. If you struggle with the regular-old congregation because it doesn't resemble what you read in Acts 2, there is a good chance you simply aren't looking at it properly.

The Church Has Me Burned Out

If some concerns keep people from joining a church in the first place, other concerns afflict ex-church members, those who have drifted away or "burned out." Interestingly, their complaints also echo the idea that the standard, traditional church isn't like the biblical church. Talk to them and they will almost certainly speak about church politics and power cliques; the pervasive sinfulness of church power structures and systems; personality conflicts with bad pastors; the stifling institutionalism and officialism of the church body with its meetings, offices, and votes; the frustration of volunteering and working hard for years with nobody else stepping up to the plate and helping; the feeling of not being welcome or fully a part of the fellowship; and a host of issues involving scandal and abused authority. Such ex-members claim that the church just doesn't seem like the continuation of the Book of Acts, featuring the followers of Jesus joyously and selflessly doing good works.

Christianity marches on as it ever has, the living continuation of the Acts of the Apostles.

To the degree that our congregations really are as described by ex-members, we need to take the complaints to heart and try to do better. But are we really so different from the Christian congregations of apostolic times? Take a look at one of the first accounts of the Early Church in Acts 6:1: "Now in these days when the disciples were increasing in number, a complaint by the Hellenists arose against the Hebrews because their widows were being neglected in the daily distribution." Translation: *The Early Church was full of sinners, and as it got bigger, it could not operate the same way it had when it was only 120 people. Specifically, the growing Church featured a power clique of insiders, the Hebrews, who were the first to become Christians, and the Hellenists (or Greeks, but probably referring to anyone who wasn't a Hebrew by birth), who had joined but then weren't being treated fairly. God is the defender of the fatherless and the widow, so the Church, in God's name, provided for the widows and orphans among them. But because of their prejudices, they weren't doing a very good job of it; they were blatantly favoring the in-group.*

"And the twelve [apostles] summoned the full number of the disciples [the congregation] and said, 'It is not right that we should give up preaching the word of God to serve tables' " (v. 2). Translation: *The people called by God to be formally and officially in charge emphasized that preaching and teaching was their main job. Thus it was decided that the practical issues of making things happen according to that teaching—in this case, making sure the distribution of food to widows was fair—should be handled by others.*

"Therefore, brothers, pick out from among you seven men of good repute, full of the Spirit and of wisdom, whom we will appoint to this duty" (v. 3). Translation: *We will institute an official office in response to this problem. This office will be formally established and have qualifications that not everyone meets. These members of the fellowship, though full* of the Spirit like the apostles, will not be apostles themselves but hold a different, humanly established office that assists the apostles.

The apostles continued, "But we will devote ourselves to prayer and to the ministry of the word" (v. 4). Translation: *Not everyone in the Church has the same job, and even though feeding the widows is incredibly important to all of us, it is even more important that the leaders of the fellowship of Jesus' followers remain devoted to prayer and the ministry of the Word.*

"And what they said pleased the whole gathering, and they chose Stephen, a man full of faith and of the Holy Spirit, and Philip, and Prochorus, and Nicanor, and Timon, and Parmenas, and Nicolaus, a proselyte of Antioch" (v. 5). Translation: *The solution involves church politics. The problem involved the Jewish insiders being treated better than the Greek outsiders, so now the men in charge of handling this all have Greek names. The outsiders have ownership and responsibility.*

"These they set before the apostles, and they prayed and laid their hands on them" (v. 6). Translation: *The twelve remained formally in charge but commissioned their brothers, who themselves were every bit as "saved" as the apostles, to hold a specific office with a specific, formal job description.*

"And the word of God continued to increase, and the number of the disciples multiplied greatly in Jerusalem, and a great many of the [Jewish] priests became obedient to the faith" (v. 7). Translation: *God was not thwarted by the sinfulness of His people and their bad behavior, but He worked through imperfect leaders, official meetings, and valid complaints, to establish formal offices filled via obvious church politics that nevertheless helped the people of God fulfill their mission.* Thus, even though the Church of Acts 6, being much larger, didn't necessarily look the same as the Church of Acts 2, it nevertheless remained the same Church it was in Acts 2 and a continuation of the same growing family of God.

Conclusion

The Church of the early twenty-first century also remains the same Church as in Acts 2 and Acts 6. Yes, things like clergy rosters, voters' assemblies, elders' meetings, budget proposals, capital campaigns, building maintenance, and all the other things that "afflict" modern churches might not excite you much, but God's people are still God's people and still doing God's work. And if you are part of the family, a member of the Body, then such things are just a part of being who you are, much like pitching in with household chores is tedious but just a part of the glory of family life.

Many ex-church members who, for whatever reason, got fed up or bored with church life probably had never really looked at their plain old congregation as the continuation of salvation history in a particular place. Newer members should take care to not make the same mistake. Yes, your pastors and elected lay leaders are sinners. Yes, the Church so very rarely looks like what it is—the children of God, the communion of saints. Because when we go by sight, it just looks like a bunch of everyday sinners. Yes, pleading for money to pay the gas bill is nobody's favorite thing to do or listen to. Yes, generous people who give of their time, money, and energy will probably get taken advantage of, as they always have been everywhere you go. But none of these are good reasons to disconnect yourself from church life.

A congregation doing Word and Sacrament ministry may not seem like the most exciting or relevant thing in your town, but when you understand it in light of God's Word and see it for what it is, you realize what a blessing membership in such a congregation is for the people of God. Christ is the Head of the Body, and we are individually members of that Body. And Christ's Body, the Church, remains alive and active in the world as the members receive Christ faithfully and build one another up in love. It might not always look like much, but such ministry is the most important thing in the world.